M000049847

J

THE SHEEP

BY
MARK E. AHLSTROM

EDITED BY
DR. HOWARD SCHROEDER
**Professor in Reading and Language Arts
Dept. of Elementary Education
Mankato State University**

PRODUCED AND DESIGNED BY
BAKER STREET PRODUCTIONS
Mankato, MN

CRESTWOOD HOUSE
Mankato, Minnesota

LIBRARY OF CONGRESS CATALOGING IN PUBLICATION DATA
Ahlstrom, Mark E.
  The sheep.

  SUMMARY: Introduces various kinds of wild sheep, including the bighorn, Dall, and Stone sheep.
  1. Mountain sheep--Juvenile literature. (1. Mountain sheep. 2. Bighorn
sheep. 3. Sheep) I. Schroeder, Howard, II. Title.
QL737.U53A38   1984   599.73'58   83-25215
ISBN 0-89686-248-8 (lib. bdg.)

International Standard Book Number:	Library of Congress Catalog Card Number:
Library Binding 0-89686-248-8	83-25215

CRESTWOOD·HOUSE

Hwy. 66 South, Box 3427
Mankato, MN 56002-3427

TABLE OF CONTENTS

INTRODUCTION:

"I wanted a picture of that ram so badly I could have run a four-minute mile to get it," said naturalist Roy Poage. "He had a curl and a half. When I was younger, I may have shot his daddy or his grand-daddy, and they were big. But this ram was bigger, and I didn't want to kill him — only take his picture."

Poage followed the Rocky Mountain bighorn ram off and on for three years.

"The knuckles and knees I skinned! The pants I ripped. I **deserved** a decent picture of that critter. Never saw more than his backside — usually going uphill. Part of his left horn had been shot away. How he lived for as long as I knew him, I don't know."

Poage finally found the ram. It was dead, at the bottom of a chasm around fifteen hundred feet deep. "It was around the middle of December," he said. "Old Daniel (I named him after my father who was a tough critter himself) probably had been driven off a cliff by another bighorn ram that was younger and stronger.

"Old Daniel wasn't very good to look at then," Poage said. "Just the same, I took the parts of him I could to study. I found that he'd been wounded at least twice by hunters." The wounds had healed and had not slowed down the ram. Poage could testify to that. He never could catch up to Old Daniel!

The Rocky Mountain bighorn is like all wild sheep of North America. The areas where they live have made them very tough and very sneaky. They are masters at staying hidden to avoid danger. In most cases, only people with strong legs and hearts will ever get close enough to photograph a wild sheep.

—M.E.A.

A bighorn ram rests near a mountain pass in the Canadian Rocky Mountains, Alberta, Canada.

Wild sheep live in high country.

CHAPTER ONE:

A look at wild sheep

No matter where they are found in North America, wild sheep live in the high country. Even those that live in the desert prefer the higher altitudes. Biologists have identified two main species, or types, of wild sheep: the Dall *(Ovis dalli)* and the bighorn *(Ovis canadensis)*. There are several subspecies, or varieties, of each type. The most common wild sheep are the Dall itself, the Stone (a subspecies of the Dall), the Rocky Mountain bighorn, and the desert bighorn. All four can be identified by the huge, curling horns of the adult males, or rams. These are the wild sheep we will focus on in this book. In this chapter we'll take a general look at wild sheep. In later chapters we'll take a closer look at the most common varieties.

Wild sheep come from Asia

All wild sheep are thought to be related to Asian sheep. Biologists believe that many thousands of years ago, many land animals, including wild sheep, migrated across a land bridge that once connected the U.S.S.R. and Alaska. The theory is that the wild sheep slowly moved south along the mountains of western North America. They spread as far south as Mexico. The various types of sheep adapted to fit the habitat in which they found themselves living.

The sheep living in a land of snow and ice in Alaska and the northern Rockies of Canada are Dall sheep. They are almost snow white. The bluish to black colored Stone sheep are found mostly in the dark mountains of British Columbia, Canada.

The wild sheep in the Rocky Mountains of southern Canada and the United States are brown. The desert bighorns found in the southwestern United States and Mexico are light tan. The coloration of the sheep allows them to blend with their surroundings. This makes it possible for the sheep to hide from danger.

Size, hair, and horns

Wild sheep usually are larger than their domestic "cousins." An adult ram, or male, in his prime can measure almost six feet (1.8 m) from the tip of the nose to its rump. The largest rams can weigh three hundred pounds (136 kg) or more. Males usually grow larger than females, or ewes. Like domestic sheep, they live in herds.

Wild sheep, however, do not have a coat of wool like domestic sheep. Instead, they have a covering of long, hollow hair to protect them during the cold winter months. The sheep shed their winter coat in the spring, and grow a shorter coat for the summer.

Both rams and ewes grow horns, but the ewes' horns remain small and sharp. Ewes have been seen using their horns for defense. Rams use their horns

Deep groves in the horns of the ram, called "growth rings," show age of the sheep.

for defense and to fight other rams. The horns of the ram begin as small spikes in their first year, and they don't stop growing during their lives. Growth rings are formed on the ram's horns. They are much like the growth rings on a tree. A deep groove is formed in the horn each fall, when growth stops. By counting the grooves, you can tell the age of the ram. If the food in its range is good, a wild ram's horns can reach a half-curl in three years and a full curl in seven or eight.

A ram with a full curl is usually seven or eight years old. This is a Rocky Mountain bighorn.

"Curl" is a term used to tell how far around the horn has grown. When the tip of the horn grows to a point even with its base, a ram is said to have a "full curl." The record for the longest horn taken from a Rocky Mountain bighorn ram is around fifty inches (12.8 cm). The horn was measured along the outside edge of the curl.

Strong & quick

Both rams and ewes are strongly built. Since their range is mostly up and down, their bodies are well adapted to climbing. They have non-skid pads on their hoofs. The pads give them footing even when racing up rocky slopes covered with moss. The sheep use their ability to move around easily in rough areas when escaping from their predators.

Many animals that live in the mountains move with careful steps. The wild sheep do not. Movement of a sheep is often a series of scrambling leaps. They have been known to quickly climb almost-vertical, rock cliffs. It would take an experienced rock climber many minutes, if not hours, to do the same thing. Sheep also will go down steep slopes in a series of leaps. A jump of fifty feet (15.2 m) down is not unusual. Within a couple weeks of being born, the young of the bighorns, called lambs, can follow their mothers almost everywhere at the same speed.

Wild sheep don't always run from predators. An Alaskan naturalist once watched a fully-grown Dall ram face an angry bear. He reported that the ram, in two charges, butted the bear so hard that the bear turned and ran. It is the impact of the butt, and not any sharpness in the horn, that does the damage.

Sheep live mostly in the highest country of their range. Few predators like to live that high. Eagles have been known, however, to attack and sometimes kill young sheep. In the northern ranges, wolves and bears have made occasional sheep kills. To the south, mountain lions and coyotes may attempt to

The wild sheep's best defense is to run. This herd of ewes and lambs ran off when they heard the clicking of the photographer's camera.

kill a bighorn. When cornered, heavy horns and slashing hoofs are the wild sheep's defenses. Its best defense, however, is to run.

The sheep is well-equipped in other ways to deal with its predators, too. Among all mammals, the wild sheep's eyesight may be the best. They can see great distances from their high pastures. A sheep will be gone long before a predator — whether man or animal — gets close. On level ground the sheep may be able to run in short bursts of thirty-five miles per hour (56.5 km per hour). Senses of hearing and smell are also well-developed in wild sheep.

Spring & summer

A spring or summer's day for wild sheep involves eating and loafing. They feed mostly on tender grasses, green twigs, flowers, and even berries. The herd will usually take its first meal in late morning. It feeds again in early afternoon, and also before bedding down at night. In between times, the sheep may bed down in a shady or sheltered area. Being a ruminant animal, the bighorn uses this time to chew its cud.

How far the sheep roam depends on how far they must go for food and water. Being bothered by people also causes them to move more. Where herds receive complete protection, like national parks, they may stay in an area only a mile or two (1.6 - 3.2 km) across. Twenty-five miles (40.3 km) would probably be an average distance for sheep to move. Desert bighorns may have to go even farther. They may need to go a long way between seeps and natural water basins if rainfall is in short supply. Desert bighorns also have to cover more ground to find enough food.

Except during the late-fall breeding season, ewes and rams live apart. The ewes and the young sheep "herd up" in one area. The older rams form "bachelor herds" and roam more freely about their range.

Lambs are born in late spring. Before giving birth,

the ewes each find a secluded spot away from the herd. This reduces the chance of a predator being able to find and kill the baby lambs. Each ewe usually gives birth to one or two lambs. Biologists think that the number of lambs born depends on the condition of the sheep's range. If food is plentiful, and the sheep are not being crowded by other animals, ewes will usually give birth to two lambs. On the other hand, if there is a shortage of food and space, only one lamb may be born. If there are severe shortages, the ewes may not give birth at all. This is nature's way of protecting the herd. By keeping down the numbers of sheep in an area with food shortages, it allows the existing sheep to survive. If the numbers of sheep increased, the entire herd might die of starvation.

After a few days the ewes return to the herd with their new lambs. The lambs quickly adapt to their mothers' diets, but they continue to nurse into the fall. When lambs get older they are called "kids." The ewe-kid herd often is governed by a "grandmother." She is usually the oldest ewe still able to bear young. Other ewes may even leave their kids under her protection to move off and graze! This is much like humans who use grandmothers and grandfathers to take care of their children.

In the bachelor herd, spring and summer are days to get ready for the coming mating season. Young rams, and even some of the older ones, have been

These young rams are playing butting games.

seen during the summer playing "king of the hill." One ram will claim the top of a small hill and dare others to knock him off.

As fall approaches, the rams begin to get restless. And what, for them, was play during the rest of the year, gradually becomes serious combat. When the mating season gets close, the "king" will be the ram with the largest number of ewes in his "harem."

Fall & winter

When fall turns to winter, normally in late November and December, the fighting between the rams increases. In each fight, the two rams square off as far as fifty feet (15.2 m) apart. They may snort and paw the ground. Then, as if they were given a signal, the two rams charge squarely at one another, meeting head (or horns) on. They come together with a crash that can be heard for miles on a crisp fall day. Then they back off and do it again. Shock waves can be seen moving through their bodies when they collide with each other. Chips and splinters may break off and fly from their horns. Blood comes from their eyes and noses as the battle goes on. It's common for the fight to last for an hour. The fight continues until one of the rams gives up or is injured.

Rams have special equipment that helps prevent serious injury during these head-to-head battles. Instead of a single layer of bone in their skulls like most mammals have, sheep have a double layer of bone. For added strength, small bones connect the double skull. The wild sheep also have an extra strong tendon in their necks. The tendon connects their head to their spine, and makes it possible for their necks to absorb the heavy blows of battle.

During the fights, other members of the herd — ewes, younger rams, and the young born earlier in the year — may be nearby. They show no interest in the battles. In time, the ram who has beaten and chased away all the other rams collects his "harem" of ewes and goes off to mate. Once mating is finished, the old rams regather, peacefully, in their bachelor herds. The ewes, lambs, and young rams, also go their own way. They won't really meet again until the next mating season. Mating usually is finished by mid-January.

Ewes are thought to be ready to mate at the end of their first full year. But for the rams it is a different story. It may take several years of unsuccessful fighting before a young ram is able to win his first "harem." In one study done on Rocky Mountain bighorns, a naturalist reported that almost ninety per cent of the lambs in one herd were sired by a single ram. The ram was a "full curl" adult that was about seven or eight years old.

Wild sheep, when food supplies are good, can live as many as fifteen years. But most wild sheep live for only eight to ten years. The rams don't have many years to be "king of the hill."

Hunting

Young sheep of all kinds have proved to be easy to study during much of the year. They seem, to those who have studied them, to be quite intelligent. The

These ewes and their lambs were photographed on a highway in Alberta, Canada. Old rams won't usually get this close to people.

older they get, the more wary of people they become. This is especially true for the rams. Because it is only legal to hunt mature rams (those with a three-quarter or better curl), the older rams wise-up quickly. They seem to know when the hunting season is coming and move into very remote country. By the time hunting season arrives, the hunter needs a good pack horse or two, perhaps another horse to ride, and a couple weeks of free time.

In most areas, hunters also need to hire experienced local guides. Without the guides, they may never see a legal-sized sheep. They may have to "pack in" to an area for a day or two before they even reach the range of the bighorn. And even when they get into the high country, it may take days to find a ram. The more the sheep sense danger, the higher and farther away they move. That makes for even more hard work for the hunter and guide. If they should get lucky and shoot a ram, just getting a heavy trophy sheep out of the remote area can take days.

To the serious hunter, the work is worth it. The wild sheep with a big set of horns is a prized trophy to have mounted. Its meat is a treat to be enjoyed with family and friends.

The hunting of all wild sheep is now carefully controlled. Hunting is allowed only when there are too many wild sheep in one area. Hunters are told exactly where to hunt.

In many areas a special drawing is held for the limited number of licenses available. Game managers throughout the range of the wild sheep want to make sure that not too many rams are harvested.

A closer look

Now that you know some things about wild sheep in general, it's time to take a closer look at each of the four main types: the Dall, Stone, Rocky Mountain bighorn, and desert bighorn.

A trophy Dall ram.

CHAPTER TWO:

Sheep of the far north

To see Dall and Stone sheep, people must go north. The common range of the Dall sheep extends from Alaska, through the Yukon, and into the

A herd of Dall sheep rams moves to lower ground.

northern areas of British Columbia. The Stone sheep is found in the south-central part of the Yukon and northern British Columbia.

Both subspecies are somewhat smaller than their southern cousins, the bighorns. Average Dall and Stone rams only reach two hundred pounds (91 kg). The average adult is thirty to forty inches (103 cm) tall at the shoulder. Dall sheep are white or sometimes slightly yellow. The darker Stone sheep are

known as "black mountain sheep." They range in color from dark gray to almost black. Except for the color of their coats, the Dall and Stone Sheep look and act very much alike. Although herds of both types have been seen close by one another, they apparently do not mate with each other.

If any one wild sheep has to live through extremes of weather, the Dall has the worst. Winter temperatures through its range stay below zero for extended periods of time. It often has to dig through deep snow to get its food of dead grass and plants. But summers in "the land of the midnight sun" are kind to the animals. The snow melts and lush green mountain meadows provide the food they need.

One of the larger herds of Dall sheep exists within the boundaries of Mount McKinley National Park in Alaska. Summertime visitors can see them playing on the slopes from a long ways away. They appear as moving white snowballs against the rocks or grass of the mountains and hills. It seems that the Dalls are naturally curious. They will come close to people on foot. However, experts who have studied them say they're always ready to turn and run. Lambs are said to be the most curious. A warning snort from an older and wiser ewe will chase the lambs away if they get too close to danger.

Predators in the range of the Dall and Stone sheep include wolves, bears, and lynxes. Of the three, the wolves may kill more sheep than the others. Hunting

Dall and Stone sheep live in some very steep country!

The horns of this mature Dall ram are more slender than the horns of a bighorn ram.

in packs, they have been seen stalking Dalls many times. More than one angry sheep, however, has "turned the tables" on a pack. With a sure-footed charge, they have been seen knocking wolves off a mountain ledge to their deaths.

In general, these northern sheep spend their summers in the highest mountains in their range. Winter drives them down the mountains to areas where it is not so cold and the snow is not so deep. Then they can use their hoofs to paw away snow and get at food.

The horns of the Dall and Stone sheep are somewhat lighter and more slender than those of the bighorns. Still, the horns of a mature ram can grow to "full curl" and beyond. The horns also flare out more to the sides, like a corkscrew.

Like the bighorns in the South, the Dall and Stone sheep mate in December after the males have had their battles. One Dall ram was seen winning a harem of almost fifty ewes! It is not unusual, however, for a ram that loses a battle to raid a large harem and run off with one or two ewes. If he's caught by the "master," however, there will no doubt be another fight.

Dall and Stone sheep live in some of the wildest country left on the continent. They have not had to put up with people, as have the Rocky Mountain and desert bighorns. Still, a lack of understanding and, perhaps, pure greed helped create a decline in their population. One naturalist reported, in the 1920's, that a group of hunters from the "lower 48" states killed almost thirty rams. That was the entire male population of one Dall sheep herd. Reproduction in that herd suffered for several years afterward. The careful work of game managers has rebuilt the herds to healthy levels in most areas.

The Dall and Stone sheep share a small part of their range with another wild sheep which is blue-gray in color. This subspecies of the Dall sheep, called the Fannin, is a prized trophy among hunters.

A Stone sheep grazes in a mountain meadow.

CHAPTER THREE:

The sheep of the western mountains

From the earliest days of the American West, the legends of the Rocky Mountain bighorn sheep have grown. At first, the stories were told by the "mountain men." Hunters, nature lovers, and people who have settled within the range of the sheep have added to the legend.

One story is told of several bighorn rams which were surprised at a watering hole. They could have run away into a valley below the hole. Instead, in a series of jumps they went from ledge to ledge on both sides of a waterfall and escaped over the top. Actually, it was instinct that made them do it. Few predators, including people, could follow them up such a steep slope.

Among the wild sheep, the Rocky Mountain bighorn is usually the largest. As was said earlier, the males weigh up to three hundred pounds (127 kg). Adults stand between thirty-six and forty-two inches (92-108 cm) tall at the shoulder. They have brown coats with white rump patches. The horns of the old

29

The bighorn has a big white patch on its rump.

rams are large and heavy. The horns of one trophy taken by a hunter weighed almost thirty pounds (14 kg). That was as much as all the bones in his body! The tips of the horns are often broken off. Some are broken in fights, and some are broken on purpose. The rams have been seen wedging the tips between rocks, and then breaking the tips off. Biologists think that the sheep do this when their vision gets obscured by the tips of their horns. This usually happens when they reach a full curl. The favorite areas of this wild sheep are high mountain meadows throughout the Rockies. When naturalists talk about the "Rocky Mountain" sheep, they usually are talking about all the sheep that populate mountain ranges in the western United States and Canada. If there are differences in size or color, they are small.

Life in the old west

Before the white man arrived in the American West, the sheep were plentiful. They had a wide range in the foothills of many mountain ranges. Early Indians hunted them and enjoyed the flesh of the sheep. The huge horns of the adult rams were used in the Indians' ceremonial dress. One Indian legend tells of how the Great Spirit arranged a marriage between the bison (or buffalo) and the eagle; the mountain sheep resulted. In many ways, the story is good. The bighorn, when rushing up or down the slopes, often seems to be flying. And yet, the bighorn is as solid as the bison.

At one time, millions of bison roamed the flatlands of the West. As Americans moved west, great herds of bison were easily killed by market hunters riding horses or even railroads. Biologists believe the bighorn was nowhere near as plentiful as the bison. But the hunters also killed very many of the wild sheep. More importantly, however, men began to graze their cattle and sheep on lands the bighorns had used for years. Being too wary to mix with the domestic animals, the bighorns usually moved up into the mountains where the food was less plentiful. With less food, reproduction slowed. In most areas of its original range the bighorn just disappeared.

On occasion, natural disasters hit the Rocky Mountain bighorn too. Ezra Poage, a mountain man in the 1840's, told in his journal about seeing a small flock of sheep buried in an avalanche of snow. The deaths of the sheep were a good thing for Poage, however. In cold storage under the snow for almost two months, they provided food and warm pelts for the mountain man. For awhile, at least, Poage didn't have to live on rabbits. In time, a group of coyotes found the cache of sheep, too. Then Poage had to share!

Running his traplines through the Rockies, mostly in Wyoming, Poage had plenty of time to watch the bighorns. In one part of his journal, dated August, 1858, he told of having a brief romp with a small group of bighorn kids: "They were playing around one or two females when I came over the ridge. The old sheep were asleep or didn't care. As I stood there one young kid came right at me and hit me in the knee. Knocked me almost down. The other kids thought that was fun. They kept trying until one of the old sheep got up and snorted. Then I didn't see them any more."

Elsewhere in his journal, Poage told of finding an

This Rocky Mountain bighorn kid is about six months old.

injured yearling ram and taking it "home." (Poage had no "home" as such. During his time in the mountains he lived in tents and caves. Once every two years, or so, he visited relatives in western Nebraska. When he died is not known. It is assumed he died in the Rockies of Wyoming or Colorado, sometime in the 1880's. His remains were never found, but one of his journals ended up in his family's hands. — the author) The young bighorn ram, he wrote, took to living with him "right well," but "took to liking" the ewes in a flock of domestic sheep nearby. The bighorn ram, larger and stronger than the domestic rams in the flock, eventually was shot by an angry sheepherder.

Rocky Mountain bighorns have, perhaps, had the most problems of all the wild sheep. Even domestic sheep seem to do well in the high country, and once the West was settled, huge flocks of domestic sheep were driven into the highlands every year. With them came diseases the bighorns had never known before. The bighorns had no natural immunity to them. Once the diseases were given to the bighorns, they died off rapidly. One of the worst epidemics to hit bighorn herds was one brought on by lungworms, which are common in domestic cattle and sheep. Domestic animals are immune to the effects of lungworms, but wild sheep are not. In the 1930's, pneumonia caused by lungworms almost wiped out Rocky Mountain bighorns in America.

Rebuilding the herds

In the early 1900's hunters and interested people decided to try to rebuild the herds of Rocky Mountain bighorns in the United States. They saw to it that strict hunting controls were started. Some areas were closed to hunting.

The big problem was getting herds started again in areas where they had disappeared. Sheep will not colonize, or move into new areas, like other wild animals. Deer, for example, will move into new areas on their own, if a herd gets too big. Young sheep, however, follow their elders. Herds have been in the same areas for hundreds of years. If a herd gets too big for its range, ewes give birth to fewer lambs. Wild sheep will not move out of their range. The only way to get sheep into a new area is to put them there. That is what was done.

Bighorns were live-trapped in places, like British Columbia, that had some to spare. The sheep were released in areas of the United States that formerly had sheep. Concerned people and game departments dropped food to the sheep from airplanes during severe winters. Generally, the program has been successful. Many western states now have expanding herds. This makes it possible to do more transplanting of the sheep to new areas. Even with this success, populations of Rocky Mountain bighorns are only about one-tenth of what they were before the West was settled.

Rocky Mountain bighorns eat many things. They have been seen licking up sap dripping from evergreen trees in the spring. To get at the sap, they had butted the trees until a "blaze", or scar, occurred in the bark. This allowed the sap to drip freely. With their sharp hoofs, they also dig up tender roots in the spring. Sheep have been seen scraping mossy lichens off rocks, too. As flowers bloom, the bighorns

Sportsmen and women help bighorn sheep survive by building feeding stations. This station was set up in the spring after a hard winter.

may eat them. The blossoms of wild clover are a favorite. When various kinds of berries ripen, they will help themselves when they can.

Almost all species of wild, vegetation-eating animals want one more thing in their diets — salt, in some form. Outcroppings of minerals occur all over their range and the animals go to these "licks," as they are called, for supplies of these minerals. Many licks contain standard salt, or sodium chloride, as well as the other helpful minerals.

Modern threats

As in the past, the biggest threat to the Rocky Mountain bighorn is people. Logging and mining in wilderness areas are the main problems. The making of access roads, the building of fences, and more people in the wild country, have hurt the populations of bighorn sheep. The sheep tend to avoid man and his machinery. They are forced into ever smaller areas. Until recently, this was a problem only in the United States. It's slowly becoming a problem in Canada, too.

CHAPTER FOUR:

The desert sheep

At a quick glance, the desert bighorns look much like their Rocky Mountain cousins. There are differences, however. They are smaller. Mature rams seldom exceed two hundred pounds (91 kg). Most adults stand only thirty-five inches (89 cm) tall at the shoulder. They are not as fat as the Rocky Mountain bighorn, but there is a benefit to their being lean. It gives the desert bighorn a large surface-to-weight ratio. This helps them get rid of body heat — which is a good thing if you live in desert areas!

The desert sheep are also usually lighter in color. This helps them blend with their paler desert habitat. And finally, the horns of the desert rams are more slender and flare out a bit more than the Rocky Mountain sheep.

Generally, the range of the desert bighorns picks up where the Rocky Mountain bighorns leaves off. The desert sheep make their homes where timbered mountains give way to lower, treeless mountains and hills. The areas they live in are arid, which means that they are hot and dry. The desert sheep seek out the highest and most rugged areas.

In the United States, desert sheep live in the dry areas of Nevada, Utah, Arizona, New Mexico, California, and Texas. There are large numbers of the animal "south of the border" in Mexico.

Life in the dry country can be hard. As the land dries, the sheep must make do with dry grasses. They also have been seen pawing the ground to get at the still-damp roots of plants which have gone dry above the surface of the earth. One of the desert sheep's more important adaptations to its environment is that it can go for much longer periods of time without water. They have learned to get some water from cactus plants. Still, the desert herds usually stay close to watering holes. The frequent shortage of adequate

Desert bighorns are usually lighter in color than Rocky Mountain bighorns. This ram is shedding its "winter coat".

food and water has limited the numbers of desert sheep.

But the rains do come to the dry deserts. When they do, it's a feast for all the animals which live there. When it rains, the deserts bloom soon after. Seeds and roots which have lain dormant in the ground suddenly burst forth. Food is abundant for a short period of time. The rains also bring some danger, particularly to the young. Sudden downpours in desert areas can bring instant floods. Desert bighorns have been known to be washed away, or drowned.

After a rain, even the desert blooms!

Predators and games

Although mountain lions and coyotes sometimes prey on the desert sheep, they are more likely to seek smaller animals. One naturalist did record an attack by five coyotes on an old ewe. One of the coyotes kept the ewe busy in front, darting in and out. The rest of the pack slashed at her hindquarters. Once crippled by the attack from the rear, the ewe had her throat slashed by one of the coyotes. The coyotes fed, then left, and returned to feed once more. In less than twenty-four hours the ewe's carcass had been picked clean by a parade of smaller mammals and birds. In nature, not much goes to waste.

Predators of the desert bighorn usually show more interest in the sheep during the lambing season. They then go after newborn lambs and ewes which are weakened by the process of giving birth. The ewes, however, seek out high, remote areas to give birth. These areas aren't easy for the predators to reach.

Biologists note two other adaptations that the desert bighorns have made. The first is that mating takes place as early as July. This allows the lambs to be born during the cooler winter and spring months. The cooler temperatures mean less stress for both the lambs and the ewes, giving them a better chance of survival. The second adaptation is that ewes seldom give birth to more than one lamb each year. This helps prevent too many sheep from competing for the limited amount of food and water.

Life for the desert bighorn is not always tough. Like the sheep in the mountains of Canada and Alaska, desert bighorns have been seen at play. Even in the desert, the adult sheep play chasing and butting "games." One observer watched a small herd of rams, most of them two to four years old. They were

The horns of a desert bighorn ram are usually more slender than the horns of its Rocky Mountain cousins.

sliding down a steep slope covered with small, shiny pebbles. When each hit the bottom of the slope, or stopped sliding, he raced back to the top and slid again. The "game" lasted for nearly an hour! Then the herd moved off to feed.

Rebuilding the herds

During the settling of the American West, the desert bighorns suffered the same people-caused problems as the Rocky Mountain bighorns. They disappeared from many parts of the original range. A more recent problem has been an increasing number of wild burros. The burros compete for the same food and water as the sheep. The burros have been forced out of their natural areas by people and domestic livestock. No one has decided what to do about the burros. But the sheep are being transplanted with fairly good success. The desert bighorns are being live-trapped and moved to new areas in many parts of the southwestern United States. Their numbers are slowly increasing. The Mexican herds have been holding their own, because they have large areas of wilderness.

CHAPTER FIVE:

At one time, the populations of wild sheep were stable all over the continent. In areas outside of the United States they still are.

In the United States the wild sheep have had problems surviving. Railroaders building their tracks across the high country of the West in the 1800's, told stories of being watched by huge herds of curious bighorns. An occasional sheep was shot by the railroaders to provide a banquet for the workers. But, as the railroads opened the western United States the real problems began.

The railroads made it possible for people to have huge cattle and sheep ranches. The cattle and sheep began to compete with the bighorns for range and for food.

The bighorns fled into an ever-smaller range to avoid people. They took with them diseases for which the wild sheep could not be treated. Epidemics swept the wild herds. It was not until populations of the bighorns seriously declined that anyone did much about it.

Until this century, not much was known about the sheep, or their habits and habitat. It was the hunting guides of the West, along with the easterners they guided on hunts, who began the effort to save the bighorns. Many of them just stopped hunting. States and provinces also began to regulate the number of sheep that could be killed. In some areas, hunting was banned entirely. People began to study these animals, to see what could be done to help them.

By the 1920's, populations of existing bighorns seemed to be stabilizing. Some herds seemed large enough that specialists herded and trapped bighorns. The trapped sheep were moved back into areas where they once had lived. These new herds grew.

In the last three decades, however, bighorns have had to face new threats. People seeking new sources of oil, timber, minerals, and ores have been allowed to enter the bighorns' range again. Even the Dall and Stone sheep, in their remote territory, have not totally escaped people exploring for natural resources

The future of the wild sheep is cloudy. In most areas, the populations remain stable. The key to their future, according to naturalists, is space. As long as we grant them space, the sheep have the chance to survive in good numbers.

MAP:

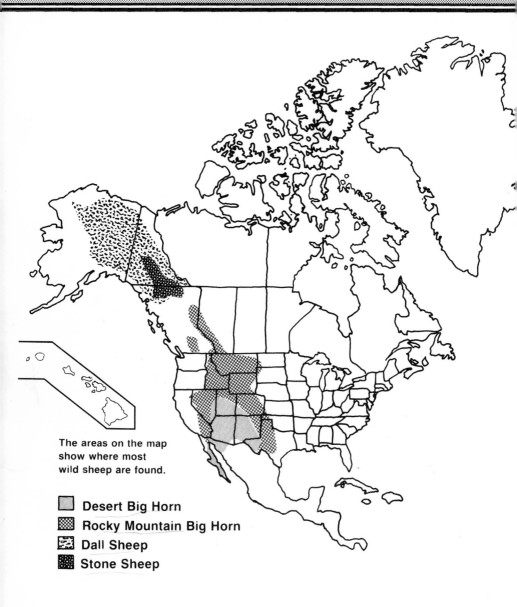

The areas on the map
show where most
wild sheep are found.

▨ Desert Big Horn
▩ Rocky Mountain Big Horn
▨ Dall Sheep
▨ Stone Sheep

INDEX/GLOSSARY:

WILDLIFE
HABITS & HABITAT

READ AND ENJOY THE SERIES:

WILLIS TARVER ELEMENTARY
3500 Summit Grove Parkway
Thorton, Colorado 80241